PYTHON

The Python Quickstart Guide

ETHAN SANDERS

CONTENTS

1
Why Learn Python

Learning to program can open an unlimited number of doors and is one of the very smartest things you can do to improve yourself right now.

Of course this is true from a career perspective first and foremost: there are countless employers out there right now looking for people who know how to code and this is something that is only going to grow more and more over time. If you can program, you can walk into nearly any job.

Or you might choose not to get a job at all... Because as a programmer, you'll be able to build tools, games, apps and more that people can enjoy and that you can charge a lot of money for! And this is a great way to make a living from the comfort of your own home.

Or maybe you'll just program as a tool? When you can program, you can build things that you *need*. That way, you can automate jobs and save yourself a huge amount of time.

And it's also incredibly fun and incredibly rewarding. Programming is a great way to challenge yourself, to train your brain to think in new ways and to get a sense of satisfaction from creating something from scratch and seeing it come to life.

Programming lets you turn pure ideas into things you can actually use – and that basically gives you unlimited potential.

But why *Python* specifically?

Well, Python just so happens to be the perfect 'gateway' programming language for beginners. It's very simple to get started with and incredibly easy to understand even with no background knowledge (unlike Java for instance). But at the same time, it's also a programming language that you can actually *use* and do useful things with. This isn't a learning tool or a 'watered down' programming language. This is a *full* programming language that just so *happens* to also be easy.

Need more proof? Then consider all of the awesome pieces of software that have been written in Python. Including:

- YouTube
- Dropbox
- Google in parts!
- Spotify
- Reddit
- EVE Online
- Pinterest
- BitTorrent (in the early days)
- Quora
- Instagram...

The list goes on. But suffice to say that some of the most successful software *in the world* is built in this very easy to learn code.

What you might also notice is that these different examples are all incredibly versatile. Python can be used to make web 2.0 apps but it can also be used to make 3D games and cloud sharing software that runs on the desktop.

Once you learn Python, you will have no limits in terms of what you create.

Heck, with EVE Online, someone created an entire 3D alternate reality that has recently seen the world's first 'digital war' erupt. Imagine what *you* could build.

Excited yet? Then let's get going…

2
Getting Started

Now I could go into detail about the history of Python but that wouldn't really be that useful. Instead, let's dive straight in and get building some useful software!

One thing we *do* need to do first though, is to install the interpreter and IDE. I should probably also tell you what those words mean…

IDE basically stands for 'Integrated Development Environment'. This is a piece of software that contains all the components you need in order to start making and testing your programs. This includes an interpreter, which basically interprets the code you're inputting so that it can be made into useful software. You'll also get a compiler that can turn your program into an executable, meaning it can run on its own ready for distribution.

The good news is that interpreters are easy to come by for Python because it's a popular language. A lot of HP computers actually come with Python already installed for instance while there is an interpreter also available from the Windows 10 Store. Max OSX comes with versions of Python too from 10.3 (Panther) and upwards.

If you decide to install an interpreter the old fashioned way though – which is probably the best way to go ahead – then you will want to download either Python 2 or Python 3. Each version has its own pros and cons but it's worth sticking with 3 for now. We'll talk about the pros and cons of each later on but suffice to say that Python 3 is the most recent version (released in 2008) but is also undergoing development still. For the most part, the two versions are very similar so if you decide to switch later on you'll be able to do so without too much trouble. Just to confuse matters by the way, these two versions are often called 2.x and 3.x…

So head over to this page and install the latest version for Windows: https://www.python.org/downloads/windows/

Or here for Mac OSX: https://www.python.org/downloads/mac-osx/

The Installation Process

Once you have the installation file, double click on it and Python will install completely on its own!

But once that's done, you might find things are still a little confusing. At this point you have something called the '**Python Command Line**' and '**Python GUI**' on your computer. If you open these, neither has any option to 'run' an app or to do any of the things you might associate with programming.

And this is where getting the IDE with a compiler built in becomes necessary.

There are actually a few different IDEs you can use and you can find a selection of those here:

https://wiki.python.org/moin/IntegratedDevelopmentEnvironments.

Some of these IDEs are free, while others will cost you money. One example is Wing IDE 5, which you can download from Steam for a free five-day trial. If you choose to pay for it though it is going to be a little pricey starting at over $70! Other options include NetBeans, LiClipse, Komodo, PyCharm and more. PyCharm is free and open source and is a very popular option among many.

You can get PyCharm here: https://www.jetbrains.com/pycharm/.

Whichever you choose, you'll now be able to launch the software and have somewhere to enter the code. And when you run the program, the interpreter will kick in and you'll be able to see it working!

But for now we're not going to be using an IDE at all. Rather, we'll be looking at how you can create apps using the **Python GUI**, which is also called **IDLE**. So find this on your computer (it should be in the start menu once you've installed the interpreter) and let's get started…

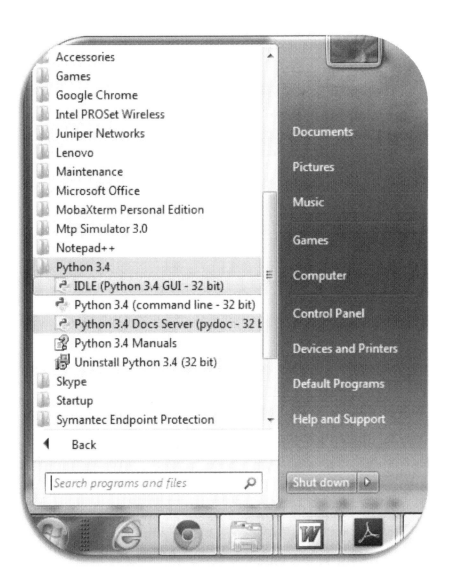

3
Hello World

It is tradition in the world of programming to start every new programming language the same way – by writing a program to say 'Hello World'. This is the most simple and straight forward program you can make and it teaches you the very basics – like how to actually get some code to run.

So how do we get 'Hello World' to run in IDLE?

Simple: we type:

```
print("Hello World")
```

And then hit enter!

Note that we're using lower case for the word 'print'. This is important as otherwise Python might think we're referring to a variable – more on that later!

Oh and one *more* note is that this may not work if you're using other versions of Python. If you get an error, try this instead:

```
print "Hello World"
```

If this works, then you might want to go back and reinstall a newer version of Python – at least the most recent Python 2!

On doing this, IDLE will seem to 'respond' by saying 'Hello World'. Simple!

But of course a program needs to be more than one line long… so how can we do that?

Well, at the moment IDLE is in 'interactive' mode. We want to change that and put it in 'script' mode so that we can write a program. To do that, we need to create something called a **module**. We'll go into what this means in more detail in the future but for now, just know that you'll need to create a new file and save it with the extension '.py'.

Just like a '.txt' file is a text document and '.mp3' is a music file, '.py' is a Python file. And when you open one of these in IDLE, it knows to be in 'script' mode.

To create a module/.py file, simply go to the 'File' option in IDLE's menu and then select 'New'. This will automatically open a new window where you can type in script mode. You can then click 'save' to save the file, and call it whatever you want leaving the extension as .py.

So now we're going to put the same code in here:

```
print("Hello World")
```

But this time we're going to run it in the Shell! To do that, just click Run > Run Module. This will then bring the interactive window back to the foreground and you'll see it say 'RESTART' with your output (Hello World) underneath. The Restart line simply indicates that a new program has run, in case you'd done something previously.

Note that you do need to *save* your script before you can run it however.

Oh and if you want to do this quicker next time, you can simply hit 'F5' to run your code!

4
Operators, Operands and Operations

Let's take a moment to reflect on what just happened there… You just wrote your own program! You are now officially a 'programmer'… so congratulations!

So what's next? Well, we start making more *useful* programs of course!

And the first and most obvious way to begin doing that is by using operators, operands and operations. This means essentially that we're going to be using Python like a big calculator!

Doing this really couldn't be easier either. If you want to do a sum in Python for example, you simply *type* out a sum! So that means you might write:

```
10 + 2
```

Now just hit return in interactive mode and you'll see the number '12' pop up on the screen. Success!

Likewise, you can also use subtraction like so:

```
10 - 2
```

Things do get a little different though if we start using multiplication and division. That's because you represent a multiplication with a * rather than X and you use / to perform division. Other than the syntax though, this is basically the exact same process.

But you will notice *one* unusual bit of behavior when you use division: the result is always shown with a decimal point! So instead of saying *5* you would see *5.0*.

This is because the division operator return what is known as a 'float' which basically means a number with a decimal point. You can remember this by thinking that a float has a decimal point that 'floats' somewhere on the screen.

If you want a round number – an integer – then you need to use another type of operator called 'floor division' (the other kind is sometimes referred to as 'true' division). When we use floor division, we actually use two slashes like so: '//'.

We'll come back to integers and floats soon when we start talking about variables. If you don't get it just yet then don't worry, it will all make sense soon!

First, lets consider a few other bits of math. If we can have '//' then can we have '**'? Yes indeed but this actually does something different! This is what's referred to as 'times times' but is more technically called 'exponentiation' and it basically means you're performing the operation multiple times. So:

```
5 ** 3
```

Actually means:

```
5 * 5 * 5
```

Something else that you'll find useful to understand is what is known as 'operator precedence'. What is this referring to? Basically, it means the order that the operations are going to get carried out.

Think about this a little like being served drinks at a bar. When you're ordering, it's always polite to ask for the most complicated drink first. So you ask for the martini shaken and not stirred with the slice of lime, *followed* by the beer. This is precedence.

In Python, precedence means that your interpreter (our bartender) is going to carry out some of the functions before others. This doesn't mean that you have to carry out those particular functions first – actually it means the precise opposite thing so it's okay to write the operations in any order that you like.

For example, if we write:

```
1 + 3 * 4
```

What would the result be? It all depends on which operation is first. Because if the multiplication comes first then you have 13. If the *addition* comes first then you have 16!

So place your bets: which do you think it is? And the answer is that the multiplication comes first! But as with any mathematical equations, we can change the order by using parenthesis (brackets). Anything in brackets will happen *before* anything else. And yes, you can have brackets inside other brackets! But just to know the order that Python does things in automatically, it is: (), **, *, /, +, -.

Okay so at this point, you have written hello and used Python like a fancy calculator. That's not terribly exciting but don't worry – things are just about to get a lot more impressive and useful! That's because we're going to be introducing one of the main concepts that is used across all of programming: variables.

5
Introducing Variables

Variables are one of the key components of any programming language and are what allow us to do all kinds of incredible things with just a few lines of code.

So what is a variable?

Well, if you think back to your high school math, then you may actually recall using variables back then. And variables in Python work in the *exact* same way.

Essentially, a variable is a container or a representative. This is a word or a letter that *represents* a number. That number can change but you can write the letter or word at any point in your math to represent it. You can think of it almost like a box and every time you tell the code to look inside the box, it will find the information you put in there. That means you can change the information regularly (by changing the value of the variable) but Python will still always know where to look!

So if you cast your mind back to your school math days, then you may recall seeing things like this written:

10 + x = 13

Find x.

In this case, 'x' is actually '3'.

This works in just the same way in Python except there's no 'finding' of x involved. Instead, we're telling Python what x is and then referring to it later. So how do we do this? Pretty simply actually:

```
x = 3
```

We could also say:

```
MyVariable = 3
```

So let's open up the script mode and try using this in part of a little program. Just write:

```
MyVariable                    =                    3
print(MyVariable)
```

Now save the program and go to run it. When you do this, you'll find that it simply outputs the value of the variable – which in this case is "3".

We haven't actually explained what 'print' does yet but by now you should have been able to work it out. This is simply a command that writes text to the screen and you can make it anything you want it to be by using quotation marks as we did when we wrote "Hello World".

But you may have noticed that we didn't *need* to use the quotation marks when using the variable. That's because the quotations marks are only there to say 'write this text exactly'.

Integers, Strings and Floats Oh My!

The variable *MyVariable* contains the number 3 with no decimal places. Thus we call it an integer. In other words, we name our variables after the data they contain. So seeing as the number '3.72' is a float, we would call a variable that contained that number a float as well!

So far so easy... But things are about to get significantly more complicated as there are a lot more types of variable and it will pay to at least be familiar with most of these...

The integer and the float are both considered 'number variables'. That means that they contain numerical data.

Actually though, there are also two *more* types of variable. These are the 'long' and the 'complex'. You'll use these two less often but essentially longs are used when you need really long numbers and complexes are used when you need very complex numbers.

So you don't need to worry about that. What you definitely *will* come across in your coding travels though is the 'string'. A string is another type of variable but it isn't numerical. Rather, strings contain letters or words. So a string could be 'a' or it could be 'Adam'. If we say:

```
MyString = "Hello World!"
print(MyString)
```

Then the program simply prints 'Hello World!' to the string just like before. Only now we could change the value of 'MyString' and the output would change. This is very helpful when we want to use the same string in lots of places but may need to change the string. For example, we could use a string if we wanted to refer to a user by name in our app. We could assign the name to the string at the start of the app and then easily refer to them using that name elsewhere.

All of the variables we have looked at so far have one thing in common – they hold one piece of data or a single value. There are also other types of variables however that contain *more* than one piece of data. So if we think of our strings, integers and floats as boxes, then these variables are more like filing cabinets, folders or bookshelves.

The standard data types available when using Python then are:

- Numbers
  - Integers
  - Floats
  - Longs
  - Complexes
- Strings
- Lists
- Tuples
- Dictionaries

For now you don't need to learn about lists, tuples and dictionaries but if you just can't wait then skip ahead to the called 'Advanced Variables'.

Performing Operations on Variables

Remember how we said that variables allowed our programs to change? That's because we can change the value of the variable whenever we like throughout our code.

As we've already seen, we can set the value of a variable very simply like so at the start of our code:

```
MyNumber = 3
```

But if we later want to change the value of our number we can simply change it *again* later on. For example:

```
MyNumber = 3

print(MyNumber)

MyNumber = 4

print(MyNumber)
```

If you run this program then it will simply output '3' and then '4'. Like so:

But likewise, we can also change our variables using the very same operations that we used in 4. For example:

```
MyNumber1 = 3
```

```
MyNumber2 = 4

MyNumber3 = MyNumber1 + MyNumber2

print(MyNumber3)
```

Can you guess what this will output?

Or how about:

```
MyNumber1 = 3 * 2

MyNumber2 = 4

MyNumber1 = MyNumber2 - 3

MyNumber3 = MyNumber1 + MyNumber2

print(MyNumber3)
```

You can even let a variable refer to itself. For example, what do you think this line of code does:

```
MyNumber1 = MyNumber1 + 1
```

Essentially, this increases *MyNumber1* by '1'. So you are saying that the value of the variable will become whatever it is right now *plus* one.

Right now this might all seem a little strange but as we go through and look at the different commands you can use in Python it should start to make a lot more sense!

The next question you might be wondering is whether or not you can also do this kind of thing with strings? And the good news is that you can and it actually works just the same! Of course you can't *multiply* a string by a string (because that doesn't mean anything!) but what you *can* do is to add two strings together to create a new one. For example:

```
FirstName = "Bill"

LastName = "Gates"

FullName = FirstName + LastName

print(FullName)
```

You'll see why all this is important soon!

(Actually, I wasn't being strictly honest when I said you couldn't multiply a string. In fact, writing *FirstName = "Bill" * 10* would make a string with the value "BillBillBillBillBillBillBillBillBillBill"!)

6
Naming Conventions and Comments

Variables are one of the most common elements in programming because they allow things to change in a controlled manner – thus allowing for dynamic programs that change over time or in response to input.

One way in which variables are different in other programming languages though, is that they must first be defined. In Python, we can simply say:

```
x = 3
```

At any point in our program and then 'x' will be created with the value '3'. In Java though (another popular programming language), x would first have to be created with a statement like:

```
Int x;

x = 3;
```

Part of the reason for this is that other programming languages use a much wider range of variables – such a 'Booleans' which can only equal one or zero. Because Python only has a few types of variable, it doesn't need as much structure.

Python affords us a little more flexibility and saves time by removing the need for defining variables but it can also lead to more confusion in larger programs. When writing lots of code, it can be useful to keep a note of what all your variables are called and what they do!

What's also important though is to think carefully when naming your variables. The objective here is to write our code in such a logical and elegant way that a complete stranger could instantly know what it does – that will help if you ever need to collaborate on a project, or if you come back to old code you've written.

When using variables in Python, it's a good idea to use proper case. We've seen that commands like 'print' are normally lower case, so if we use proper case or capitals for our variables, then they will stand out very easily when reading through.

So if you are using a string to refer to a user's name, then what should you call it? A good option would be: *UserName* or *Name*. This will make life much easier than if you call it *Rabbit1112*…

Another tip is to try and choose variables that *read* well as though they were written in English when they're inserted into the code. We'll touch on this more in future.

Using Comments

To make finding your way around just that little bit simpler, note that you can also use comments. 'Comments' are lines of plain English that you can insert into your code. The compiler will ignore these lines when you run your program but it means you can add instructions, notes and references for yourself or other members of your team.

To insert a comment, simply precede your line with a '#' symbol. The comment will then extend to the very end of the physical line. If you're coding using IDLE, then the comment will instantly change to a red font when you get it right:

Think ahead while writing your programs as taking a little time to keep your code clean now can save you a real headache later on

7
Handling Inputs

At the moment, all the programs we've written do is to output information. As you can imagine… this isn't very useful! If you've never written code before, you might even be wondering why any of this matters. After all, if you wanted to say 'Hello World' you could just write it on a piece of paper…

To solve this problem then, we need to start inviting the user to join in and actually interact with the software we've written. One way we can do this is with the command 'input'. The great news is that input is actually very easy to use! Essentially, this just lets the user assign a value to a variable.

So instead of saying:

```
UserName = "Bill"
```

You say:

```
UserName = input("Please enter your name: ")
```

This now means that the program will add a prompt asking the user to enter their name:

Once the user acquiesces to our request, *UserName* will then equal whatever they said. This means we can say:

```python
UserName = input("Please enter your name: ")

print("Hello " + UserName)
```

Now, whatever the user says their name is, we can greet them using it! Congratulations are in order: you just created your very first interactive program!

(**Note** that if you're using Python 2, you'll need to use *raw_input* instead of *input*. This is our first example of where Python 2 and Python 3 differ – but it's no biggie!)

So what else can we do with this? Well of course we can also use the input command in order to capture and set other types of data. Such as integers!

For example:

```python
UserAge = input("Please enter your age: ")

print("You are ", int(UserAge))
```

In this example there are a couple of other things going on but you can probably work out some of it.

First of all, we're creating a string called *UserAge* just as we did before. The 'prompt' is asking for the age and input will automatically be converted into an string.

From there, we are then printing the output. Note that we can't use '+' when adding a string to an integer, so instead we're just using a common to list both values one after the other.

And next, we are converting the value that user gave us into a string by using the *int(UserAge)* line. You can also convert integers into strings by saying *str(Number)*. This way you could convert 4 into "4".

Let's have a bit more fun and see what we can do with this information and a little math...

```
UserAge = input("How old are you? ")

print(int(UserAge), "is sooo old!")

YearsTo100 = 100 - int(UserAge)

print("In ", YearsTo100, "years, you'll be a
hundred!!")
```

Now you have a program that is basically very rude about your age and that tells you how many years until you're 100. Nice!

Or what if we take it one step further?

```
UserAge = input("How old are you? ")

print(int(UserAge), "is sooo old!")
```

```
YearsTo100 = 100 - int(UserAge)

print("In ", YearsTo100, "years, you'll be a
hundred!!")

print("That is ", int(UserAge) * 360, " days!
Or ", (int(UserAge) * 360) * 24, " hours.
Man...")
```

That extra line means it can now tell us how many hours and days we've been alive. I'm 28, which I'm informed is 10,080 days or 241,920 hours.

The program might be a little offensive… but it's also starting to pull together quite a few different things we've learned! At this point we're able to accept input to create new variables, then perform operations with those variables and present an answer on the screen!

8
Loops

Input is one of the most useful operations you'll find yourself using at first when you program. But this is still only scratching the surface of what you'll be able to do as you learn more and more Python.

Another powerful tool for instance is to use loops. Loops essentially allow a piece of code to keep running and repeating itself.

There are two different types of loops, which operate based on different conditions. One of the most common examples of a loop for example is the 'While' loop. The clue as to how this loop works is very much in the name. Basically, a while loop runs *while* something is true.

So for instance, we could say:

```
Number = 0

while Number < 100:

    Number = Number + 1

    print("Counted to", Number)
```

All this would then do is to print numbers from 0-100 on the screen. The *while* command is followed by a conditional statement (*Number < 100*) and everything that follows the colon and is indented will then happen while that loop runs. If we remove the indentation, then this signifies that we have come to the end of the loop. So the final line in this section of code will only show once the loop has completed:

```
Number = 0

while Number < 100:

    Number = Number + 1

    print("Counted to ", Number)

print("Finished and counted to 100")
```

Leaving a space between the lines makes no difference.

This is another situation where it becomes *very* important to be careful with formatting and planning. Simply pressing backspace and accidentally deleting an indentation is enough to prevent the code from working properly! This is quite different to other types of code such as java or C# where the loops are contained within curly brackets {*like this*}.

Note that if we hadn't included the line *Number = Number + 1* then the loop would have run forever!

The other type of loop we can use is the 'For' loop. For basically performs some kind of counting job and finishes once that job is over. For example, this:

```
for Counting in range(100):

    print(Counting)
```

Does the same thing that the previous loop did – counts to one hundred! But we could also do something else interesting – for example we could do this:

```
for Counting in range(10, 100):

    print(Counting)
```

And thereby count from 10 to 100!

This is another example of something that might seem rather pointless currently. Why would you want to count to 100 this way when you have other methods? Well, one example might be to look through a list of items – and we'll discuss that in the on 'Advanced Variables'.

What else can you do with loops? Well, one option is to 'break' the loop. This simply terminates the loop early and then continues with the rest of the program. This can be used in the 'while' and 'for' loops and is something we'll come across later on...

One way that it might be useful as an example though, is if we use *while True*. This statement (notice the capital 'True') simply runs our loop until we say otherwise with *break*. We'll use this in the very next chapter...

Another one that will come in handy is 'continue'. This works similarly to the 'break' statement, except that it simply begins the loop again from the start. And if you were 'For' loop, then the condition that you were testing would also be reset. Again, it will all make perfect sense soon…

9
If, Then Statements

At this point we've already gone over a lot of the most important components of any programming language. Variable, loops and operations are all crucial for any program and inputs also play an important role a lot of the time.

But there is perhaps nothing that characterizes programming as a whole quite as well as the 'IF, THEN' statement. This is a little sequence of code that basically tests a condition and produces output based on that. The result is an instruction that reads 'if this, do that'.

For instance then, we can allow a user only to progress when they've answered a question correctly, or when they have entered the correct password.

But before we get onto that, there's one more thing you need to know about...

Comparing Variables

We're going to carry on with If and Then in a bit but before we do, there's one more thing to consider: comparing variables.

Sometimes it will be useful to look at one variable and then compare that to another variable. For instance, we might want to compare a string to a stored password if we're asking someone to log in. Alternatively, we might be trying to find out if someone is older or younger than a certain age.

To do this, we have a few symbols and conventions. To ask if something 'equals' something else, we will use the symbol '==' (using '==' compares two variables, whereas one '=' forces them to be the same). This is what will allow us to test certain conditions for our IF, THEN statements. This way we can say 'IF' password is correct, 'THEN' proceed.

For example:

```
Password = "guest"

Attempt = "guest"

if Attempt == Password:

    print("Password Correct")
```

This essentially tests the imaginary password attempt against the true password and only says 'correct' when the two strings are the same. Notice that we aren't actually using the word 'next' at any point. In some programming languages (such as BASIC) you actually do write 'next' but in most it is implicit. Anything that comes after the colon is next, which is just the same way that loops work! Python is nice and consistent and it's actually a very attractive and simple language to look at when you code with it well...

(That's right – programming languages can be attractive! In fact, there is even such thing as 'code poems'!)

We can also use an input to make this a bit more interactive!

Doing this is very easy:

```
Password = "guest"

Attempt = input("Please enter password: ")if
Attempt == Password:

    print("Password Correct")
```

Try entering the right password and you should be presented with the correct message – congrats!

There's just one problem at the moment, which is that our user will still be able to get into the program if they get the program wrong! And there is nothing to tell them that they answered incorrectly…

Fortunately, we can fix this with our next statement: 'else'.

As you might already have guessed, 'else' simply tells us what to do if the answer is *not* correct.

This means we can say:

```
Password = "guest"

Attempt = input("Please enter password: ")if
```

```
Attempt == Password:

    print("Password Correct")

else:

    print("Password Incorrect!")
```

Note that the 'else' statement moves back to be in-line with the initial 'if' statement. Try entering wrong passwords on purpose now and the new program will tell you you've made a mistake!

Okay, so far so good! But now we have another problem: even though our user is entering the password wrong and being told as much, they are still getting to see whatever code comes next:

```
Password = "guest"

Attempt = input("Please enter password: ")if
Attempt == Password:

    print("Password Correct")

else:

    print("Password Incorrect!")

print("Secret information begins here...")
```

Of course this somewhat negates the very purpose of having a password in the first place!

So now we can use something else we learned earlier – the loop! And better yet, we're going to use *while True*, *break* and *continue*. Told you they'd come in handy!

```python
Password = "guest"

while True:

    Attempt = input("Please enter password: ")

    if Attempt == Password:

        print("Password Correct")

        break

    else:

        print("Password Incorrect!")

        continue

    print("Secret information begins here...")
```

Okay, this is starting to get a little more complex and use multiple concepts at once, so let's go through it!

Basically, we are now starting a loop that will continue until interrupted. Each time that loop repeats itself, it starts by asking for input and waits for the user to try the password. Once it has that information, it tests the attempt to see if it is correct or not. If it is, it breaks the loop and the program continues.

If it's not? Then the loop refreshes and the user has another attempt to enter their password!

We've actually gone on something of a tangent here but you may recall that the title of this was 'Comparing Variables'. What if we don't want to test whether two variables are the same? What if we want to find out if one variable is bigger than another? We can ask if something is 'bigger' using the symbol '>' and ask whether it is smaller using the '<' symbol. This is easy to remember – just look at the small end and the big end of the character!

Adding an equals sign will make this test inclusive. In other words '>=' means 'equal or bigger than'.

Likewise, we may also test if two strings are *different*. We do this like so: '!=' which basically means 'not equal to'.

Using that last example, we can turn our password test on its head and achieve the exact same end result:

```
Password = "guest"

while True:

    Attempt = input("Please enter password:
```

```
")

    if Attempt != Password:

        print("Password Incorrect!")

        continue

    else:

        print("Password Correct")

        break

    print("Secret information begins here...")
```

Of course when you get programming you'll find much more useful ways to use this symbol!

Elif and Or

Else is one more command you need to learn to use If statements properly. Equally important though is 'Elif'. Elif is essentially a portmanteau (two words combined) of the words 'Else' and 'If'.

So what we now have is a statement that gives the following instruction:

'If this is true, do this' (IF)

'If that's *not* true, but this is, then do this' (ELSE IF – ELIF)

'Or else, do this' (ELSE)

So what might this look like? Here's a little example of some code that talks to you differently dependent on your gender. You might find that this also contains another new word you're not familiar with...

```
Gender = input("Are you male or female? ")

if Gender == "male" or Gender == "Male":

    print("Hello sir!")

elif Gender == "female" or Gender ==
"Female":

    print("Hello ma'am!")

else:

    print("What is one of those?")
```

The new word in question is of course 'or'. Let's see how all this works...

Basically, our program is asking you to tell it if you're male or female. If you say male, it calls you sir. If you don't say male but you *do* say female, then it says 'hello ma'am'.

If you say something else entirely though, then it gets a little confused and asks what you just said.

The 'or' meanwhile, let's us perform the same if either one of two statements is true. In this case, we're allowing the program to proceed with either the lower case 'female' or proper case 'Female'. There are other ways to do this but this is a good way to demonstrate the power of 'or'.

If it weren't for or, we would be forced to do this:

```
Gender = input("Are you male or female? ")

if Gender == "male":

    print("Hello sir!")

elif Gender == "Male":

 print("Hello sir!")

elif Gender == "female":

    print("Hello ma'am!")

elif Gender == "Female":

    print("Hello ma'am!")

else:

    print("What is one of those?")
```

This is another good demonstration of how some code can be more elegant than other code. You might wonder why it matters but when you come to look back over this and you have to sift through thousands of lines, it actually makes *all* the difference. Moreover, reducing the amount of writing you have to do will save you time and energy – and will also mean the programs you write actually run more quickly!

Let's Make Our First Game!

We've talked an *awful* lot of theory at this point so perhaps it's time for us to make our first game! It's not going to be that much fun, seeing as you'll know the answer – but you can get your friends to play it to impress them with your coding know-how (unfortunately, it's still not all that fun even then!).

The game is simply going to get the player to guess the number it is thinking of and will then give clues to help them get there if they get it wrong.

```
CorrectNumber = 16

while True:

    GuessedNumber = int(input("Guess the
number I'm thinking of!"))

    if GuessedNumber == CorrectNumber:

        print("Correct!")

        break
```

```
elif GuessedNumber < CorrectNumber:

    print("Too low!")

    continue

elif GuessedNumber > CorrectNumber:

    print("Too high!")

    continue

print("You WIN!!!")
```

Nesting Ifs and Loops

It's also possible to 'nest' your ifs and your loops in order to make even more elaborate programs that test multiple different conditions.

We already did this once when we put the 'if' inside the loop. However we can also put ifs inside ifs inside ifs if we want!

10
A Brief Interlude – Thinking Like a Programmer Part One

Let's take a breather and have a moment to discuss the power of conditional statements (another term for 'if' and 'then') and how it affects programming in Python – as well as programming in general.

Essentially, these kinds of statements are going to form the backbone of your programming and will be what you use to inject *logic* into your programs. We'll learn a little about adding graphics and doing other fancy things later – but ultimately the logic is what makes a program tick.

For instance, if we were making a platform game then it would be an 'if' statement that would make the character fall *if* the ground wasn't underneath them (it could also be done with a while statement but that's not really the point!).

Pseudocode

Something else you need to learn about programming at this early stage, is that probably 90% of it is done *away* from the computer. What do I mean by that? Simply that you'll work out how you're going to apply your logic when you're washing up or when you're driving. All you do when you're sitting down is to *execute* that idea by writing it down.

For this, you'll find something called 'pseudocode' comes in handy. What this basically is is a kind of 'mental shorthand' for your programming that allows you to wrestle with ideas without needing to write actual code. It's also useful for communicating with other coders, for grasping concepts and for explaining code to people who use other languages like Java.

To write in pseudocode, simply name variables in a descriptive manner (with no need to explain how you got them) and forget all about formatting conventions.

To demonstrate, this is how the 'physics' of our aforementioned 2D platformer would work in pseudocode:

```
    While Y-coordinate-underneath-character is
EMPTY:

    Y coordinate = Y coordinate + fallspeed

    Else:

    If player-presses "right" then:

       X coordinate = X coordinate + walkspeed

    Else IF player-presses "left" then:

          #Go the other way
```

```
Else if player-presses "jump" then:

    #jump sequence

    Y-coordinate = EMPTY;

End if
```

Take a look at this code and hopefully you should have an idea of how it works and how it would enable a character to walk and jump when on a flat surface. I've used bits of formatting from Java, BASIC and Python and also written some plain English in there – but it's intuitive to understand even if you have *zero* coding knowledge.

This is going to come in handy when you're dreaming up your next big app idea and it will also help us explain concepts further in this book!

I'm actually going to demonstrate this right now by teaching you a new concept using pseudocode! That concept is 'and' – another useful command for writing conditional statements. AND basically tests *two* conditions and only runs if both of them are true.

For instance:

```
If FirstName = Bill AND LastName = Gates Then
print "You created Windows!"
```

Get it?

A Quick Lesson: Logic Gates

Just to give you a little background too, it can be very interesting and useful to get an understanding of what's actually happening behind the scenes when you create these kinds of conditional statements in your code.

Essentially, IF, THEN statements are actually representative of the underlying physical components of your device. Specifically, your computer/phone's CPU uses a complex network of switches in order to allow the creation and destruction of circuits. When you code, it gets translated by the interpreter into binary – which means 1s and 0s.

Computers understand binary code as 'on' and 'off' where 0 means off and 1 means on (take a look at the power button on your device – it's a zero with a one through it!). Your code then is turning on and off switches in order to redirect electricity and when you use conditional statements, this creates what is known as a logic gate.

What is a logic gate? The easiest way to visualize it is by imagining two straight wires both connected at either end to the same bulb and the same battery. The bulb is also connected back to the battery from the other side, completing the circuit.

But from the battery to the bulb, we have two parallel wires and two 'routes' that the electricity can take to light it. If we put a switch on both wires, then the bulk will light up as long as *one* of those switches is in the 'ON' position. We now have our 'OR' statement!

But what if we got rid of the second wire and instead put one switch after another? Now the electricity *has* to travel through both in order to light our bulb...

Which is the *AND* statement that we only just learned!

One wire with just one switch? Well, that's just good old 'IF'.

Don't worry too much if you don't get this, it's not really important. But if you do get it, you hopefully now understand a little more about how electronics actually work!

11
Advanced Variables

Alright, that's enough messing around! Back to the hard stuff...

This time we're looking at variables again – but we're going to see some of the more complicated things we can do with them...

To start with, let's take a look at how we can chop up our strings!

For instance: *print(MyString[5])* will show the fifth letter of a string and *print(MyString[0:5])* will print the first letters from your string. Likewise, you can say *print(MyString[3:10])* and print characters three to number 10!

This is where using something like a for loop can be combined with other tricks to do something interesting.

Here's a little twist on our usual 'Hello World' program:

```
for i in range (12):

print(MyString[i])
```

This still prints 'Hello World' only now it does it one letter at a time! We can use this then to search through a string to present answers to questions that don't have to be exact.

Lists, Tuples and Dictionaries...

But there are other more interesting ways to store lots of data in a variable. One example of this is to use a 'list' type variable. This simply means you have one variable that is going to contain lots of different variables in order. To do this, we create the list using square brackets and then place each item inside.

```
Listy = ["H", "e", "l", "l", "o", " ", "W",
"o", "r", "l", "d"]

for i in range (11):

    print(Listy[i])
```

This does the same thing as the previous hello world!

Of course lists tend to be put to much better use than this though! For instance, we could use them to make a shopping list:

```
Listy = ["Apples", "Pears", "Oranges",
"Juice", "Milk", "Bread", "Eggs", "Ham",
"Toilet Paper", "Washing Up Liquid",
"Toothpicks"]

for i in range (11):

    print(Listy[i])
```

This will now print out your shopping list for you!

But what if we want our list to be dynamic and respond to input? We can do this by using the 'len' command, which returns the length of our given list; and the 'append' command, which adds another item to the list.

So check this neat little program out...

```
print("Add items to your shopping list and type
'done' when you're finished!")

Listy = list()

while True:

    NextItem = input("Next item: ")

    if NextItem == "done" or NextItem == "Done":

        break

    else:

        Listy.append(NextItem)

        continue


for i in range (len(Listy)):

    print(Listy[i])
```

Now every time the user hits return, they will add a new item to their list and be prompted to add one more! They can then just type in 'done' to complete the list, at which point they'll be shown the whole thing!

Notice that in this case though we have had to define our list with the *Listy* = *list()* line. Otherwise, Python doesn't know not to treat that variable like a regular string. You don't need to do this though if you're entering multiple data sets into your list as soon as you create it.

Tuples meanwhile are a bit like lists except they're read only. And when you create them, you use parenthesis instead of square brackets. To be honest though, you're unlikely to need them for a while – so you can just stick with lists for the sake of simplicity!

More interesting though are dictionaries. These are variables once again, except this time you're giving each piece of data a 'key' that can then be used to retrieve it. These are known as 'maps' in some programming languages and basically allow you to set multiple properties for a single item. You can call the keys whatever you want and this will allow you to retrieve them logically later on. Eventually, we could create entire databases this way!

This time, we use {curly brackets}. Like so:

```
AdamData = {'name': 'Adam','age':28,
'weight': 170}

HannahData = {'name': 'Hannah', 'age': 29,
```

```
'weight': 150}

print(AdamData['name'])

print(AdamData['age'])

print(AdamData.keys())

print(AdamData.values())
```

Try running this program to see what it does. Notice that we can list the values or the keys as well as retrieving them individually!

12
Functions and Global Variables

At this point you can do all sorts of cool stuff but you might be finding it all a little underwhelming still! After all, your programs still run in this tiny little environment with no graphics... They're not online... There's nothing unpredictable about them...

Basically, you need to begin to extend your powers. And the way you're going to do that is with functions and modules!

To start, let's take a look at what a function is...

Understanding Functions and 'Object Oriented' Programming

Also known as 'classes' and 'subs' in other programming languages, these are sections of code that exist outside of the main linear flow but can be called at any point. So you could create a 'sub' that printed 'Hello' and call it 'HelloPrint()'. Then, every time you wrote the line 'HelloPrint()' in your code, it will execute that short passage.

For example:

```
def HelloPrint():
```

```
print("Hello World!")

return;

HelloPrint()
```

To create any new function, we used the command 'def' which basically means 'define' and tells Python to treat the that word as a reference to this section of code from now on. After that point, we can then refer to it whenever we want to in future.

But we won't generally do that with Python because this is an example of an 'object oriented' programming language. That means that it wants to work with data and to treat data like objects. Thus, the key purpose of using functions is to *change* data somehow. It sounds limited but actually it just requires you to think in a slightly different way – and the end result is better organized and more elegant!

This is what the brackets are for – that's where we insert the variables and/or data that we want to be transformed by the function. So for example:

```
def counter(Name):

    length = len(Name)

    return length;


NamePlease = input("Name length counter!
```

```
Enter your name ")

print(counter(NamePlease))
```

This is a piece of code that can count any name typed into it!

```
def counter(Name):

    length = len(Name)

    return length;



while True:

    NamePlease = input("Get the length of
next string: ")

    print(counter(NamePlease))
```

And now we're making more use of the function by using it repeatedly to measure any string that the user wants to count! This is an app that has a genuinely useful purpose – you could count the length of *War and Peace* if you were so inclined...

Note: You need to define your function *before* you refer to it. This is something that isn't necessary with other programming languages always but here we're treating our functions just like variables!

Global and Local Variables

Now you're playing in the big leagues and using functions to organize your code, you need to be aware of local and global variables.

Basically, a global variable is a variable that you can refer to at any point throughout a program. Meanwhile, a local variable will only work *within* a specific function. And the only difference as far as the way they're made is that variables created within functions are local and those created *outside* of functions are global.

You can access and change global variables within functions but not vice versa!

13
Modules, Graphics and More

So what does this have to do with extending your power? So far all it has done is saved you a lot of typing...

Well, the beauty of modules with local variables is that you can use them anywhere in your code and even grab them from one program and insert them into another. These work in a modular fashion and that means you can be much more efficient in the way you code – even lifting functions straight from other pieces of code in order to make use of their algorithms and sequences!

And Python is designed to make this as easy as possible thanks to its use of modules.

You see, when you create new files in Python, you're really creating new *modules*. These modules can then be treated as though they were functions within your own code!

Let's take a look at the 'game' we made earlier that let our player calculate the number being thought of. The problem with this game was that you couldn't play – because you already knew what the answer was from having made the game!

Well, how about we add a random number?

There's just a small problem though… Python doesn't include a random number generator as one of the commands! Or at least not as one of the *built-in* commands! Thankfully though, there are modules out there that you can use to access this ability.

And fortunately, one that can generate random numbers came packaged with Python when you installed it! And all you have to do to access it is to reference it as so:

```
from random import randint

print(randint(0,9))
```

This simply defines a function (*randint*) from another module and allows you to access it as though it were your own!

And now you have your random number! Notice that this function is letting us pass two different variables to it – there's no limit to the amount of data that can be passed and transformed using functions.

So let's use this in our game! It's easy:

```
from random import randint

CorrectNumber = randint(0,10)

while True:

    GuessedNumber = int(input("Guess the
number I'm thinking of between 0-10!"))
```

```
if GuessedNumber == CorrectNumber:

    print("Correct!")

    break

elif GuessedNumber < CorrectNumber:

    print("Too low!")

    continue

elif GuessedNumber > CorrectNumber:

    print("Too high!")

    continue

print("You WIN!!!")
```

You can now play this game as much as you like. See if you can work out what the fastest way to get to the answer is every time!

Turtle Graphics

Just to show you by how much you can start to improve the power of Python, check out how you can go about adding fancy graphics to your programs!

```
from turtle import *

color('red', 'yellow')
```

```
begin_fill()

while True:

    forward(200)

    left(170)

    if abs(pos()) < 1:

        break

end_fill()

done()
```

The module 'Turtle Graphics' is one that's used to teach children a little about coding and it can draw images on the screen. This little exercise combines the ability to draw with a *while true* to create a repeating pattern.

You could create an even more interesting one using the random module!

Installing New Modules

To find and install new modules for Python, you simply need to know what you want to do and then find the modules that can help you accomplish that task!

The good news is that installing modules is easy enough for the most part. Normally they're called 'packages' and while they'll be complicated to work out in some cases, for the most part the creators have given them their own installation files just like any other program for windows!

In other words, if you want to download the Pygame.py module and start creating more professional looking video games, you simply need to download the program from http://programarcadegames.com/python-3.4.3.msi (http://programarcadegames.com/python-3.4.3.msi)
and then double click on it to go through the installation instructions – just like when you installed Python in the first place! Now your interpreter *knows* how to use that code and it will automatically be referenced when you compile and run your programs.

Note that modules can sometimes be referred to as 'libraries' as well.

14
Thinking Like a Programmer Part 2

Earlier I discussed a little about the way a programmer thinks in logic and how they will 'program' even when they're away from the computer!

Now it's time to talk about another side to the programmer mindset – which is the inability to ever repeat the same process more than once! Good programming means being efficient and that means never writing anything you don't have to.

This is why it's perfectly acceptable to use open-source modules for your code and in fact encouraged by the community. You can find tons of free stuff on sites like GitHub and this way you can start coding like a pro in a record amount of time. You're not reinventing the wheel – rather you're letting a legion of talented programmers help you accomplish goals you never could on your own!

So when you want to know how to do something that wasn't covered in this book, that's what you do: you look for the command or module that can do it. Only if it isn't already there do you have to come up with the solution yourself.

This is also just the best way to learn. No programmer remembers every single line of code from every single language they know! Instead, they just copy and paste and lift and share each time they need to do something.

Half of programming is just browsing Google and copying and pasting. The rest is thinking about logical solutions to problems (the fun bit) and occasionally searching for bugs and typos (the not-so-fun bit).

So test this theory out by seeing if you can pick up the next thing you need on your own. Look for a library that will let you write to a text file, or perhaps one that will let you play an MP3 file! Just search 'How to play MP3s in Python' and you'll find a *wealth* of information there to help!

And to encourage you, don't worry too much about what you don't know. Instead, give yourself a task or a challenge of some sort and then work on solving that challenge. Come up with a project and make it your mission to make that project a reality! That way, you'll learn what you need *as* you need it. Make this something really simple to start with, but something that you also want to turn into a reality and that will motivate you to keep going.

And the first time you successfully find yourself asking a question in a forum and borrowing someone's answers... well that's when you know you're a real programmer!

There's a huge amount more to learn but now you have the knowledge and the tools to start learning it yourself. Have fun!

15
Setting Up PyCharm

We mentioned PyCharm earlier in this book as a passing interest but now it's time to actually give it a go. Writing scripts in the text editor is only going to allow you to do so much and eventually, you'll find yourself needing something a little more powerful in order to edit your work and try it on the fly. This will also allow you to view your game assets and all the files in your project and much more.

To get started, head over to the JetBrains website (www.jetbrains.com) and then download PyCharm using the link on the main page. This will then download automatically. Choose the Community version in order to get the free and basic version that will take up the least space on your computer.

Installation is super easy: just click on the .exe you've downloaded and then set a folder to install the files to. With that done, it should execute on its own and install everything for you.

Finding Your Way Around the IDE

Once that is up and running, you can simply click on the icon in your Start Menu in order to launch the IDE. Select 'New Project' and then choose the location for that project on your computer, as well as the name of the program you're going to make. For now, you can type anything in here!

Project Window

With that done, the IDE will now boot up. So what exactly are you looking at here?

What you should see, is three separate windows on your screen. On the left is your 'Project' window. This window shows you the project files, which will include any code, as well as any libraries you use and also things like graphics, sounds and more. If you right click on the project folder up at the top, then you'll find that you can create a new file, including a new 'Python File'. This of course is a file that contains script that you'll be writing, so do that right now and you'll now have somewhere that you can start writing! Call it whatever you like.)

If you want to, you can right click on the project window and select '**show in explorer**'. This will open up the folder in Windows Explorer, thereby allowing you to view and edit the files as you would any other.

Below the main folder (and now you're new file), you should find that there is another folder called 'External Libraries'. Remember in an earlier chapter, we mentioned that 'libraries' was another word for modules. Therefore, these are external packages of code that provide you with modules you can use in your own programs. We'll see in future how you can use and install these additional libraries as you go.

Something useful you can see right now though, that will actually help you to get a better understanding of how all this works, is the Python Standard Library modules. Remember earlier I mentioned that Python came with certain additional modules built-in? And we actually went ahead and used the library 'Random' in order to generate our random number? Well, if you click on the External Libraries folder, then on Python 3.6.0 (or whichever version you have installed) and then on 'Lib', you'll be able to see a large list of folders and .py files. These are our modules and libraries!

And if you scroll down the list, then you can actually see 'Random' right there – as well as 'Turtle'. If you click on one, you'll find it opens in another tab next to the blank script you've made! Don't edit these (or you'll risk damaging their functionality) but if you want to learn how to use different libraries, then looking through their code to find the different modules within can give you some idea.

On the whole though, this is some pretty high-end stuff... so let's just close that for now!

Script Window

On the right hand side, you will find that you have your empty code page (now that you've created it in the project). This is where you code and it should look a little similar to the editor we've been using through IDLE.

Something *new* though that you may not notice right away, is that our script window will show us our errors by underlining them in red. So if you type:

```
Print "You WIN!!!"
```

And you're using Python 3, then you will see that the space is underlined red. This tells you that there's something wrong with your code and you can that way edit it if you need to!

If you hold the mouse over the red wiggly line, it will even tell you something about the problem. In this case, it says 'End of statement expected'. Fix it and the red line will go away.

Another cool thing about coding here, is that you can see at a glance where all of the errors are located throughout your code. Look at the scrollbar on the right and you'll see a selection of yellow and red lines (if you have a lot of code here). Click on any of those lines and your code will jump *straight* to the line where there's a problem.

If you do have a lot of code, then you'll notice that *some* of the lines aren't red but are rather yellow. These yellow lines are areas where your code isn't *wong* per-say but could maybe be better. For example, it might be that a line isn't actually doing anything helpful. If you just write:

```
Print
```

Then there is no rule that you can't do this but it isn't actually doing anything useful. Thus, it is highlighted in yellow and if you hover the mouse over it, it will say 'Statement seems to have no effect and can be replaced with a function call to have effect.'

Finally, you might also notice that there are some blue lines down the side when you have lots of code in this window. These blue lines change position depending on what you have clicked on and the great thing about this, is that it lets you find instances of the same words.

Why might this be useful? Well for instance, if you were looking for instances of a particular variable that you created, then you could find it just once, click on it and then see where else you have used it in your code.

You can also use this in conjunction with comments to create little bookmarks throughout your code. For example, you could keep a list of modules at the top of your code as comments, then click on one to quickly jump to it when you need to.

Another neat feature is the ability to expand and compress loops and modules by clicking on the small 'plus' and 'minus' figures next to them. This can shorten your code considerably for the sake of quickly and easily flicking through.

In short, using an IDE like PyCharm will save you time by providing more powerful formatting and editing tools.

Game Window

Our final and most exciting window though is the one down the bottom called 'Run Game'. Can you guess what this does yet? Type your code into the script view and then click the green 'Play' button on the left of the Game window at any time and it will run. You can then click on it to interact with it as you normally would and this will save you a lot of time and effort versus having to save your program and run it separately every time – especially if you have multiple different .py files all working together for a single, larger project.

If this window isn't here when you first boot up PyCharm, then don't worry. You should be able to open it by heading to Run > Run 'Game'.

Note that this window will occasionally act differently, as will the main scripting console. Let's use our little graphical demo from earlier:

```python
from turtle import *

color('red', 'yellow')

begin_fill()

while True:

    forward(200)

    left(170)

    if abs(pos()) < 1:

        break

end_fill()

done()
```

Now, if you click play, you'll find that a new window breaks out of the one you're currently in and plays the demo.

So What is an IDE?

Note that an IDE is only an interface. At first, it can be all too easy to confuse an IDE with the programming language itself. But remember: you already installed Python onto your PC and this came afterward. This is simply a tool for *interacting* with Python and for giving you everything all in one place. It is an 'integrated development environment'.

To demonstrate this, whether you use *raw_input* or *input*, will not be dependent on the IDE but rather on the version of Python that you installed. And likewise, the same is true for *Print ""* or *Print("")*.

This is why 'PyCharm' makes so much sense – it is charming the snake!

This also means that you can use any one of numerous different IDEs and find the one that suits you best. Don't worry though, although we've only discussed the one, you will find that they are largely much of a muchness with the same basic windows and functionality. You can use any IDE you like but just bear in mind that it will be a little easier going forward if you are using the same interface as I will be. For its simplicity and free nature, I recommend PyCharm!

16
Making a Basic Python Game: Hangman

What is the best way to learn a new subject? One theory that is very popular among learning gurus is that the best approach is to look at something you'd like to make and then *make it*.

This is much better than trying to learn without any structure because it gives you a goal and something to work toward. Rather than learning code in a random order and trying to remember everything in a very abstract sense, creating something that is going to be actually useful or fun gives you a context and informs which things you need to learn first.

My advice to you as a beginner is to decide on something you'd really like to make, whether that's a basic game or a useful tool. Either way, you can then do the research as required to make it and by the end, you should have much more confidence ready for tackling future projects.

For now though, let's apply this principle with a very basic game of hangman. As we try and introduce some basic features for our game, we'll be going through a lot of the things we've learned so far but putting them into practical application. At the same time, we'll find that we need more and more tools and this will allow us to extend our toolset. So how is this going to work... read on and find out!

Lists Revisited

Okay, so if we're going to make our Hangman game, then probably the first thing we'll want to do is to get our game to generate a word for our player to guess.

Now, we could do this by getting the game to select from a bunch of random letters in order to make a randomly generated word. But then most of what was produced would not actually be a *word...* so for now we're just going to have to list our words.

To that end, we should create a bunch of variables and then pick from one of them using the random module.

To do that, we might begin with a list of strings and then pick from them based on the number. It might look like so:

```
from random import randint

word1 = "calculator"
word2 = "music"
word3 = "optimal"
word4 = "diagonal"
word5 = "hexagonal"
word6 = "muscle"
word7 = "irate"
word8 = "python"
word9 = "libraries"
```

```
randumber = randint(1,10)

if randumber == 1:
    word = word1

if randumber == 2:
    word = word2
```

Etc…

(Notice there's a little bit more formatting on our code now? This is what happens when you paste directly from PyCharm!)

The only problem with this plan is that… well it's *awful*. It requires *such* a lot of repetitive coding and it's completely un-scalable. If we ever wanted to be able to make a game that we could play ourselves with hundreds of different possible words, then we'd need to type out hundreds of different things.

So instead we use a list, which we learned about a few chapters back. Now, we can create something like this…

```
from random import randint

Listy = ["calculator", "music", "optimal", "diagonal",
"hexagonal", "muscle", "irate", "python", "libraries"]

word = Listy[randint(0,len(Listy) -1)]
print(word)
```

So, if we were learning for the first time, we would already have learned how to use arrays for practical benefit, as well as 'len' and the random module.

See how it all starts to come together?

If you were to run this, then you would see PyCharm output one of those words for you.

But of course we don't actually want to tell our players the word, or that kind of defeats the point! Instead, we want them to guess and in order for that to work, we need to show them the relevant number of spaces.

So to this end, we're going to add a little loop and we're going to remove the bit where we show our hand. Now the code looks like this:

```python
from random import randint

Listy = ["calculator", "music", "optimal", "diagonal",
"hexagonal", "muscle", "irate", "python", "libraries"]

Word = Listy[randint(0,len(Listy) -1)]

Rounds = 0
spaces = ""


while Rounds < len(Word):
    Spaces = Spaces + "_ "
    Rounds = Rounds + 1
```

```
print(Spaces)
```

This should output a nice selection of lines for us, with spaces in between them and this will tell us how many letters are left for us to guess. We can also add the phrase 'Guess the Word!' or something similar.

Now we want to introduce a lives system and for that, we're going to create an integer. We want to make our game hard but not impossible, so let's start with 13 – unlucky for some but also half of the alphabet!

Now we're going to give our player a chance to guess the letters in the puzzle. So let's add that element…

First, we need to create a string to represent the letter that our player is going to guess, which we can call 'LetterGuess' for the sake of convenience.

Next, we are going to input that guess using *input*. And then we're going to see if the letter that the player inputted is part of the word.

Learning Some New Tricks!

Now we're learning something new: how to check if a letter is in another word! Of course we could do this the roundabout way using a loop to check each letter individually but this would be a waste of time seeing as there is already a single line of code that will do what we need it to; and it could NOT be easier!

That word is 'in'. So just add this:

```
LetterGuess = input("Guess a letter: ")

if LetterGuess in Word:
    print("Got one!")
else:
    print("Nope!")
```

Now our game lets us guess and tells us if the guess is correct or not!

Tidying Up With Modules and Loops

But in order for that to be of any use, we also want our guesses to impact on our lives system, so that we can't just keep guessing indefinitely until all of the letters are gone! It would also be good to see some kind of feedback…

So to start with, let's introduce our 'Lives' variable and start removing points each time that we have an attempt…

We can do this simply by using Lives = Lives – 1 each time the person guesses.

We're also going to turn our spaces-drawing code into a module and we're going to introduce a variable called 'ReferenceWord'. ReferenceWord will be the name of the string that our player is going to create through their guesses. Each time the player guesses one of the letters correctly, it will be added to that reference word. Each time they fail to guess correctly, it will *not* be added. We can then compare the two words in order to draw the new image and fill in the blanks as they are guessed correctly…

So the following bit of code isn't introducing anything new that you shouldn't already be familiar with. However, you might well find that it is somewhat confusing at first – at this point we're starting to introduce a whole lot of different concepts into a single piece of code and each one will rely on the others to work effectively…

This is the code so far:

```python
from random import randint

Listy = ["calculator", "music", "optimal", "diagonal",
"hexagonal", "muscle", "irate", "python", "libraries"]

Word = Listy[randint(0,len(Listy) -1)]
ReferenceWord = ""
Lives = 13


def DrawSpaces(HiddenWord, Attempts):
    Rounds = 0
    Spaces = ""
    while Rounds < len(HiddenWord):
        if HiddenWord[Rounds] in Attempts:
            Spaces = Spaces + HiddenWord[Rounds]
        else:
            Spaces = Spaces + "_ "
        Rounds = Rounds + 1
    return Spaces;

print(DrawSpaces(Word, ReferenceWord), "\n")


LetterGuess = input("Guess a letter: ")
```

```
Lives = Lives - 1
if LetterGuess in Word:
    print("Got one!")
    ReferenceWord = ReferenceWord + LetterGuess
else:
    print("Nope!")

print(DrawSpaces(Word, ReferenceWord), "\n")
```

So what does all this do? Well, first, we have made our little bit of code that draws the spaces into a separate module. This allows us to run it multiple times but it also means that we need to pass the variables to and from it. We can't access the same global variables so instead we need to 'pass' the hidden word (the word we grabbed from our list at the start) and we need to pass the attempts we've built up.

When we guess correctly, the letter we guessed will be added to our 'Attempts'. This will then allow us to check each letter in our hidden word against our attempts. To do this, we can get the character from any string simply by using String[index]. This works just the same as it does for lists!

So:

```
word = "moose"
print(word[2])
```

Returns 'o'.

If there's a match, then the 'DrawSpaces' module will draw the letter that we correctly guessed. If there's no match, then it will continue to show a blank space!

Remember, using 'Return' in object oriented programming allows us to essentially 'code' a variable. By returning the value of 'Spaces', we can treat this just like a regular string and that means we can include it in print statements, check its length, look into its index etc. Each time we reference it though, we need to pass it the strings that it is using in its algorithms to calculate.

One more thing: note that the '\n' indicates a new line and we can use this to keep our game nice and tidy!

At the moment, our game only gives us one attempt. So it's time we put that module we created to good use by creating a loop that will let us keep trying until we guess correctly or we are out of lives...

Doing this is pretty simple:

```python
from random import randint

Listy = ["calculator", "music", "optimal", "diagonal",
"hexagonal", "muscle", "irate", "python", "libraries"]

Word = Listy[randint(0,len(Listy) -1)]
ReferenceWord = ""
Lives = 13


def DrawSpaces(HiddenWord, Attempts):
```

```
Rounds = 0
Spaces = ""
while Rounds < len(HiddenWord):
    if HiddenWord[Rounds] in Attempts:
        Spaces = Spaces + HiddenWord[Rounds]
    else:
        Spaces = Spaces + "_ "
    Rounds = Rounds + 1
return Spaces;



while Lives > 0:
    print(DrawSpaces(Word, ReferenceWord), "\n")
    print("Lives: ", Lives, "\n", "\n")
    LetterGuess = input("Guess a letter: ")
    Lives = Lives - 1
    if LetterGuess in Word:
        print("Got one!")
        ReferenceWord = ReferenceWord + LetterGuess
    else:
        print("Nope!")
```

So now we have a game that will let us guess as many times as we like! Each time the loop goes round (which continues until lives = 0), it will draw the spaces and letters and give us a chance to input one more option. We lose a life each time we guess and once we've lost all our lives, the loop stops. It would be very easy at this point to say 'Game Over!'.

But how can we reward our player for winning?

One obvious way would be to create another much larger string, which would construct our letters in order. Or alternatively, we could try and make our LetterGuess string organized in the correct order, which would require a fair amount of effort.

This is where we need to engage in a little lateral thinking though and this is a perfect example of the kind of fun thinking you can end up doing when you're a programmer!

How about you try and work it out for yourself a second and then read on once you've come up with an idea…

See, the way that *I* would approach this, is to check the string we're printing for blank spaces (the underscore character). These are eradicated each time we get a correct answer, so if we have filled out *every* letter correctly, there will be no more blank spaces left!

Remember, to bust out of a loop, we use the command 'break'. This means that we can deploy this early if we notice that the new DrawSpaces reference doesn't return any blanks!

The entire playable game should now look like this:

```python
from random import randint

Listy = ["calculator", "music", "optimal", "diagonal",
"hexagonal", "muscle", "irate", "python", "libraries"]

Word = Listy[randint(0,len(Listy) -1)]
ReferenceWord = ""
```

```
Lives = 13


def DrawSpaces(HiddenWord, Attempts):
    Rounds = 0
    Spaces = ""
    while Rounds < len(HiddenWord):
        if HiddenWord[Rounds] in Attempts:
            Spaces = Spaces + HiddenWord[Rounds]
        else:
            Spaces = Spaces + "_ "
        Rounds = Rounds + 1
    return Spaces;


Winner = 0


while Lives > 0:
    print(DrawSpaces(Word, ReferenceWord), "\n")
    if "_" not in DrawSpaces(Word, ReferenceWord):
        Winner = 1
        break
    print("Lives: ", Lives, "\n", "\n")
    LetterGuess = input("Guess a letter: ")
    Lives = Lives - 1
    if LetterGuess in Word:
        print("Got one!")
        ReferenceWord = ReferenceWord + LetterGuess
    else:
        print("Nope!")


if Winner == 1:
    print("\n You Win!")
else:
```

```
print("\n You Lose!")
```

Notice we have one more bit of code here: 'if not in'. This is literally the opposite of the 'if in' line that we saw earlier. Once again, it reads just like English and is entirely intuitive for us to know what it means. That's just one more reason that people love Python!

Some Lessons to Take Away

You can try entering this in yourself, or you can just copy and paste this code for now. Either way, you'll then be able to try tweaking things yourself or changing things to see how it affects the way the game performs.

This is also *generally* an example of good coding practice. We've done a lot with very few lines of code, which is partly thanks to the beauty of Python and partly thanks to the way that our code has been arranged. If you collapse the 'DrawSpaces' module and the loops, you'll be left with something really rather compact and elegant:

```
from random import randint

Listy = ["calculator", "music", "optimal", "diagonal",
"hexagonal", "muscle", "irate", "python", "libraries"]

Word = Listy[randint(0,len(Listy) -1)]
ReferenceWord = ""
Lives = 13
```

```python
def DrawSpaces(HiddenWord, Attempts):...

Winner = 0

while Lives > 0:...

if Winner == 1:
    print("\n You Win!")
else:
    print("\n You Lose!")
```

That is the beauty of Python!

The other reason that this game can be considered a good example of correct coding practice, is that the way it has been written means that we can now very easily and quickly grow our game by adding new words to the list. Had you created this game and released it on the Android app store, you would now be able to *very* easily apply updates by replacing the words or adding entirely new ones.

But it could be better, it definitely could be better! And that's why we're going to look at expanding the functionality even *more* in the next chapter...

16
Adding More Features and Functions

Were we to stop there, we would already have a fairly decent little game to play and we would have learned a few useful lessons.

But it's by pushing onward and honing and refining our game that we'll be able to learn even more advanced skills!

To start with, there's still a little bit of basic tidying up to do.

The first thing we need to do, is to prevent our user from entering too many characters at once. That's easy enough to do using code that we've used a few times at this point:

```
while Lives > 0:
    print(DrawSpaces(Word, ReferenceWord), "\n")
    if "_" not in DrawSpaces(Word, ReferenceWord):
        Winner = 1
        break
    print("Lives: ", Lives, "\n", "\n")
    LetterGuess = input("Guess a letter: ")
    if len(LetterGuess) > 1:
        print("Enter one character at a time! \n")
    else:
        Lives = Lives - 1
```

```
if LetterGuess in Word:
    print("Got one!")
    ReferenceWord = ReferenceWord + LetterGuess
else:
    print("Nope!")
```

Likewise, we could also prevent our player from guessing the same letter more than once:

```
while Lives > 0:
    print(DrawSpaces(Word, ReferenceWord), "\n")
    if "_" not in DrawSpaces(Word, ReferenceWord):
        Winner = 1
        break
    print("Lives: ", Lives, "\n", "\n")
    LetterGuess = input("Guess a letter: ")
    if len(LetterGuess) > 1:
        print("Enter one character at a time! \n")
    elif LetterGuess in ReferenceWord:
        print("Already guessed! \n")
    else:
        Lives = Lives - 1
        if LetterGuess in Word:
            print("Got one!")
            ReferenceWord = ReferenceWord + LetterGuess
        else:
            print("Nope!")
```

And we are reusing a previously visited line of code again here too, this time 'Elif' – which if you recall essentially means 'Else, If'.

Another safety precaution to make our game a little more fun, would be if we were to

Reading From Files

While our hangman game is quite elegant in the way that the code has been written, it is still somewhat limited. Adding new words in those quotation marks will take a lot of time and with the best will in the world, you're probably not going to sit there and write thousands of words...

Wouldn't it be better if we could play the game in such a way that we could reference an external file? That way, our players might even be able to add more words themselves. We could even have different categories of words and get the players to choose from them themselves!

This is something we can do fairly easily and the best part is that we don't even need to reference an additional library – the functionality is built right into the core of Python.

So to do what you want to do, use the following code:

```python
from random import randint

with open('D:/words.txt') as f:
    Lines = f.read().splitlines()
```

```
Word = Lines[randint(0,len(Lines) -1)]
ReferenceWord = ""
```

What we have done here, is to open the file 'words.txt' from the D:\ drive and then split it into a list called 'Lines'. We could also write lines this way and do all manner of other useful things!

Now, all you need to do is to make your text file and fill it with the words that you want to include in your game!

Now when you play the game, it will randomly pick one line from the text file and you can keep adding to these as you go.

17
Adding Additional Modules

But right now our game only runs inside the shell and this doesn't look very professional. It also means that you couldn't easily share it with friends or sell it.

The first thing we need to do to make this a lot more professional-looking then, is to add some graphics. We've seen how to make graphics with Turtle, but those graphics were pretty much just vectors created very slowly... *not really* suitable for a game that you want to become a best-seller!

So instead, we need to try using another module called 'PyGame'. And this in itself is going to be a handy learning curve because PyGame isn't actually included in the Python Standard Library, meaning that you're going to need to install it separately.

And it can be a *little* fiddly. Fortunately, I'm here to guide you through it!

Installing Additional Modules

First, head on over to PyGame.org/downloads.shtml, where you'll be able to find the download files. This is where things get a little complicated, because you need to ensure that the version you download is the right one for your particular set-up.

At the time of writing, the latest version of PyGame is 1.9.1 but there are *several* options for downloading it for Windows alone. Specifically, you need to find the closest version of PyGame for your version of Python. So as I am running Python 3.6, the closest version is PyGame for Python 3.2. I also need to ensure that I download the x32 or x64 bit version, depending on which Python installation and which PC I'm running.

Once you have the download file (.msi), you can click on it and it will install automatically. However, you need to choose the location where Python is installed on your machine. Choose the base folder and it will install the files in the right places.

If all goes to plan, then restart PyCharm. Now type:

```
import pygame
pygame.init
```

And you should find that there are no red underlines.

Problem is, there might still be. And that's where things get really fiddly and unfortunately you start to see one of the big *drawbacks* of Python. Yes, we have raved about Python a lot in this book and there's lots to love. This is a programming language that is at once beautiful, simple and a fantastic introduction to programming and to object oriented programming in particular. It's also incredibly versatile and can be made to create a wide range of different

THE PYTHON QUICKSTART GUIDE

tools (as we're going to see over the next few chapters).

BUT it is also a bit fragmented. Python is split down the middle right now with some people still using Python 2.7 and many more still using Python 3.4. Many have ignored the latest version (3.6), or chosen to stick with Python 2.7 owing to not all modules yet supporting 3.4.

That is to say, that if you have built a program that entirely relies on a module that only supports 2.7, then you wouldn't want to make the switch to 3.6 *even though* it has many superior qualities!

So what do we do?

There's a good chance that your version of PyGame won't work with your version of Python and the reason is that you are running PyGame 3.2 for Python 3.6. And if you look at PyGame.org, it hasn't been updated since *2009*.

This leaves you with two options. Option one is to uninstall Python (click on the same installation .msi file that you clicked on to install it). Now you're going to download Python 2.7 in the 32bit version and *then* install PyGame for that iteration. You'll then need to open up PyCharm and edit your code to replace your lines of code that are for the Python 3 (e.g. Print("") becomes Print ""). You'll also need to update the path, so that PyCharm knows where to find Python for interpreting your code. You'll find this by heading to 'File > Settings' and then choosing Project: Hangman (or whatever you called the file) and Project Interpreter. The line along the top on the right, should be the path of your Python installation. Once you change this, you should find that PyCharm works like a... charm (sorry, I had to).

93

This all might seem a bit fiddly but it is a useful learning curve that will show you a little more about the interaction between Python and PyCharm – and how the different versions will affect your experience.

Option two, is to use a less user-friendly method of installing modules. The good news is that this will allow you to use a version of PyGame that is intended for the latest version of Python and which is available in 64bit. The problem is that it is 'pre-release', which means that it doesn't come with the 'easy installer' (MSI file).

The good news is that you can find a *huge* repository of the latest versions of *tons* of Python modules here: http://www.lfd.uci.edu/~gohlke/pythonlibs/#pygame.

Keep this link handy, as it will come in useful a lot.

Download the most relevant file. Right now that file is 'pygame-1.9.3-cp36-pc36m-win_amd64.whl. If you're reading this some time in the future and you're running a different version of Python, then just look for the most relevant and up-to-date file.

Now take that file and drop it in your Python root folder, in the sub-directory called 'Scripts'. Hold shift and right click anywhere within that folder. This will then allow you to open up a new command line in that directory. Do that and then type: pip install pygame-1.9.3-cp36-pc36m-win_amd64.whl.

If all goes to plan, then it will install this latest version onto your drive in the correct folder. Failing that, you might need to update your 'pip', which is a package manager of sorts for easy installation.

Type 'python –m ensurepip –upgrade' and 'pip install wheel'.

Again, this is a very messy process and might be a little off-putting but it's also good practice and these kinds of skills will help you out immensely going forward.

18
Getting Started With PyGame –
Animations and BMPs

So now you should have PyGame up and running, one way or another. I'm pygoing to assume that you followed the latter process and thus are still using Python 3.6. If so, then you can follow along precisely with the instructions, otherwise, you might need to make a few changes (which PyCharm should help you with).

With that said, make a new file in your project to experiment with your game. Remember how to do this? You right click on the main project folder and then select New > Python File. Let's call it 'Graphics'.

Now copy out the following and we'll go over what it all means...

```python
import pygame

pygame.init()
img = pygame.image.load('hangmanbg.bmp')

white = (248, 248, 255)
w = 640
h = 480
screen = pygame.display.set_mode((w, h))
running = 1
```

```
myfont = pygame.font.SysFont("monospace", 50)
label = myfont.render("HANGMAN", 1, (0, 0, 0))

screen.fill((white))
screen.blit(img,(0,0))
screen.blit(label, (10, 10))
pygame.display.flip()
```

You should already be able to work out some of this. Of course the line *import pygame* is used to include the Pygame module in our code. We then need to initialize the pygame module ready for use, which we do by using *pygame.init()*.

Next, we're right away using a new feature of Pygame in order to load an image into a variable. *Pygame.image.load* lets us load images straight from the folder. Let's use this image, which is going to serve as the background for our game:

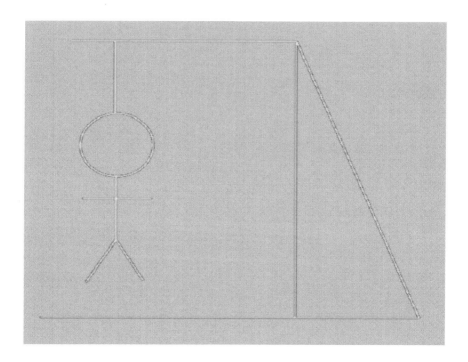

You can make your own image but note that we're going to be placing black text on top, so make it something that will allow you to read on top of!

Next, we are defining *white* and *w* and *h* (width and height) and then creating our screen. The width and height are 640x480 and note that this is also the precise size of our image, so it will nicely fill the background.

We also create a font, which we load from the system fonts and we create a 'label' which is how we are now going to show text.

Now we are telling the game to fill the background with the color we created (white) and we are telling it to draw our image at the coordinates (0,0) and we are telling it to show the text at coordinates (10,10).

Finally, we are updating the image with 'flip'. This is basically a way to update the display (you can also use *pygame.display.update()*) and until you do this, your game isn't going to show all the things you have lovingly created!

Let's test it then shall we? Save the file and then click the play button.

Aaaaand...

The old hangman game will open. What?

Thing is, when you hit play, you will simply launch whatever the *last* program you were running was – in this case the hangman game. So instead, right click on your script and then select 'run' from there. You'll now run your game which *should* open up in a new window.

Looks great right! The only problem? The game has also crashed!

Hit 'stop' and let's rectify that.

Actually, the game hasn't crashed but has 'stopped responding', which Windows tends to assume is a crash.

We can solve this little problem by adding a loop of any kind to help make the game *active* again. We do this like so:

```
Running = 1
```

```
while running:

    event = pygame.event.poll()
    if event.type == pygame.QUIT:
        running = 0
```

This now checks to see if the game is running and if so, it continues the loop. Running is a simple Boolean and as long as it =1, the loop continues. This should prevent the game from crashing and you can now drag the window around the screen as you see fit!

Animations

But there's not much point (most of the time) in having a game that simply 'stays open until it is closed'. Hmm...

So instead, we want to make our app into something a bit more interesting. You can place any other loop into the space here. For example, if you wanted to, you could make a ball that simply moved across the screen and this would look something like so:

```
import pygame
pygame.init()

black = (0,0,0)
w = 640
h = 480
x = 0
y = 240
```

```
screen = pygame.display.set_mode((w, h))
screen.fill((black))
running = 1


img = pygame.image.load('ball.bmp')


screen.blit(img, (x, y))
pygame.display.flip()

while running:
    x = x + 1
    screen.fill((black))
    screen.blit(img, (x, y))
    pygame.display.flip()
    if x > w:
        running = 0
```

Everything here you should already be familiar with. The only changes we have made are to change the background color black (and the ball has a black background too) and to set the coordinates of X and Y to integer variables. The ball then moves right across the screen until it is off the edge because the X coordinate is further than the right of the boundary. Once that happens, *running = 0* and the game automatically exits!

19
Adding Input and More

So, we've seen how to draw graphics to the screen and we have a working hangman game. All that is left to do then, is to make our working hangman game *utilize* graphics.

Now what you *could* do, is to place your graphics inside the existing modules and to replace the text outputs and inputs with labels and text rendered to the PyGame surface (we call our screen a 'surface' and yes).

But this would create several problems. For starters, there is no equivalent to the 'input' command in PyGame. After all, where would the input dialog even be situated?

To solve this problem, we could always use another module (there are some libraries for text input) but that isn't very elegant – most of these don't look all that nice and they aren't going to be as flexible. After all, when was the last time you remember inputting text that way in a game?

Instead, it would be much more elegant to simply find out what key our player was pressing and we can do that by listening for events, just as we did when we were listening for the player quitting the game. (By the way, without that line of code, we can't actually *exit* our game… so it is important!)

Remember, that looked like so:

```
Running = 1



while running:

    event = pygame.event.poll()
    if event.type == pygame.QUIT:
        running = 0
```

And this let us listen for the player pressing the cross to close the program. Now we're just going to add another event to listen for, this time the player pressing something!

```
while Running:

    while True:
        for evt in pygame.event.get():
            if evt.type == KEYDOWN:
```

This way, you are listening for the 'KEYDOWN' event and from there, we can get the value of the key pressed. We do this like so:

```
if evt.type == KEYDOWN:
    if evt.unicode.isalpha():
        LetterGuess = evt.unicode
```

This now lets us grab the input from the user and turn that into our 'LetterGuess', rather than having them type it in and press enter. This also ensures that it is only one character, that it is Unicode, that it is lowercase... it's generally much better!

We can then proceed as usual and test the letter against the original word and our correct guesses, while updating the remaining lives. Now though, we'll be outputting the information to the screen, rather than using the console.

To do this, I created new strings for Lives and for Messages (messages being things like 'Got One!' or 'Enter one character at a time!'.

I've also created a different sized font for the heading and I've used different colors for our score, our messages etc. These look like so:

```
screen.fill((248,248,255))
screen.blit(img, (0, 0))
screen.blit(titlefont.render("HANGMAN", 1, (0, 0, 0)), (10,
10))
screen.blit(myfont.render(DrawSpaces(Word, ReferenceWord), 1,
(0, 0, 0)), (10, 100))
screen.blit(myfont.render(Message, 1, (0, 255, 255)), (10,
200))
screen.blit(myfont.render(("Lives Remaining: " + str(Lives)),
1, (255, 0, 0)), (10, 300))
pygame.display.flip()
Message = "Let's Play!"
```

Now all that is left to do is to add this update within our event listener. At the same time, we also need to provide a way for the loop to quit (we use 'Pygame.quit()' in order to exit our surface and 'quit()' to exit the game altogether). I also used another new command, *time.sleep(5)*, which gives us a brief pause before showing the 'You Win!' or 'You Lose!' screen.

Note that *time.sleep(5)* requires a new dependency. This time our module is called *'time'* and it is part of the Python Standard Library (thankfully!). Import that up the top along with Random and with Pygame.

I've also used another little trick – we can only render strings to the surface (not integers) and for that reason, I've used Str(Lives) in order to convert the lives into a string.

With all that done, the final game should look something like this:

```
from random import randint
import time
import pygame
from pygame.locals import *
pygame.init()

screen = pygame.display.set_mode((640, 480))
screen.fill((248,248,255))
Running = 1
Message = ""
Winner = 0
with open('D:/words.txt') as f:
    Lines = f.read().splitlines()

Word = Lines[randint(0, len(Lines) - 1)]
ReferenceWord = ""
Lives = 13
LivesString = ""
img = pygame.image.load('hangmanbg.bmp')
```

```
myfont = pygame.font.SysFont("monospace", 50)
titlefont = pygame.font.SysFont("monospace", 70)


def DrawSpaces(HiddenWord, Attempts):
    Rounds = 0
    Spaces = ""
    while Rounds < len(HiddenWord):
        if HiddenWord[Rounds] in Attempts:
            Spaces = Spaces + HiddenWord[Rounds]
        else:
            Spaces = Spaces + "_ "
        Rounds = Rounds + 1
    return Spaces;

LetterGuess = ""

screen.fill((248,248,255))
screen.blit(img, (0, 0))
screen.blit(titlefont.render("HANGMAN", 1, (0, 0, 0)), (10,
10))
screen.blit(myfont.render(DrawSpaces(Word, ReferenceWord), 1,
(0, 0, 0)), (10, 100))
screen.blit(myfont.render(Message, 1, (0, 255, 255)), (10,
200))
screen.blit(myfont.render(("Lives Remaining: " + str(Lives)),
1, (255, 0, 0)), (10, 300))
pygame.display.flip()
Message = "Let's Play!"


while Running:
```

```python
while True:
    for evt in pygame.event.get():
        if evt.type == KEYDOWN:
            if evt.unicode.isalpha():
                LetterGuess = evt.unicode
                if len(LetterGuess) > 1:
                    Message = "Enter one character at a
time!"
                elif LetterGuess in ReferenceWord:
                    Message = "Already guessed!"
                else:
                    Lives = Lives - 1
                    if LetterGuess in Word:
                        Message = "Got One!"
                        ReferenceWord = ReferenceWord +
LetterGuess
                    else:
                        Message = "Nope!"
                screen.fill((248,248,255))
                screen.blit(img, (0, 0))
                screen.blit(titlefont.render("HANGMAN",
1, (0, 0, 0)), (10, 10))

screen.blit(myfont.render(DrawSpaces(Word, ReferenceWord), 1,
(0, 0, 0)), (10, 100))
                screen.blit(myfont.render(Message, 1, (0,
255, 255)), (10, 200))
                screen.blit(myfont.render(("Lives
Remaining: " + str(Lives)), 1, (255, 0, 0)), (10, 300))
                pygame.display.flip()
                if "_" not in DrawSpaces(Word,
ReferenceWord):
```

```
            running = 0
            Winner = 1
            screen.fill((0,0,0))
            Message = "You Win!"
            screen.blit(myfont.render("You Win!",
1, (0, 255, 255)), (10, 200))
                pygame.display.flip()
                time.sleep(5)
                pygame.quit()
                quit()
        if Lives < 1:
            running = 0
            Winner = 0
            screen.fill((0,0,0))
            screen.blit(myfont.render("You
Lose!", 1, (255, 0, 0)), (10, 200))
                pygame.display.flip()
                time.sleep(5)
                pygame.quit()
                quit()
        if evt.type == pygame.QUIT:
            Running = 0
            pygame.quit()
            quit()
```

Okay, so that's a fairly complex amount of code there but it doesn't contain *anything* that you won't already be familiar with. Take a long hard look at the code and try pasting it into your own version of PyCharm in order to see how it works. You should find that your game runs quite nice and smoothly!

Now I recommend that you try tweaking it and seeing if you can change parts

– this is how you will get a fuller understanding of how it's actually working and how you will take away some useful and useable information from it. Don't just paste this and share it – learn from it, tweak it and develop it into something completely new!

20
Creating an Executable File

Wow, would you look at how far we've come! We've gone from having a text program that runs only in a shell, to having a full-blown game that works just like any other. It opens in a separate window, draws graphics to the screen and is generally rather fully-functional!

So well done you.

But if you wanted to share or even sell a game like this, how could you? Right now, someone would need to have Python installed on their computer and then they would need to paste all the code into PyCharm...

To do this then, we need to turn our code into a single executable. The good news is that there is a piece of software that will allow us to do this and that can package everything from our graphical elements to our library dependencies all into one file!

It's called *PyInstaller* and it can be found at Pyinstaller.org.

Better yet, you can install it very simply by typing *pip install pyinstaller* into the command line! Do that and the entire thing will download and be ready to go!

There's just one unfortunate downside...

It doesn't work with Python 3.6 at the time of writing. As of *22 days ago*, the creators said that they were working to provide support, so this is something that we'll see very soon.

But in the meantime, you're going to have to roll back to at least Python 3.5 and you *may* wish to do this whole thing in Python 2.7 just to be on the safe side...

You know the drill by now, you'll need to uninstall your current version of Python and then find the 64bit version of Python 3.5 or 2.7 to replace it with.

Aaand of course you also need to install the relevant version of Pygame using the MSI or using Pip. Pip is recommended because it will automatically detect and uninstall the other versions you might have installed.

That said, it doesn't hurt to first try and remove the existing installation of PyGame yourself, which you can do by typing 'pip uninstall pygame' from the command line!

From here, you can now create an EXE of your game! To do that, all you need to do is to enter into pip again and then use the line: pyinstaller.exe --onefile --windowed "C:\Users\rushd\PycharmProjects\Hangman\Hangman.py" – replacing the file name and location with your own.

You might have difficulties if you are missing a working win32 file and there are various other things that can go wrong here too. Unfortunately, you'll just have to chase these up and again, this is one of the things that is a little more frustrating about using python. Like I said before, it's a fantastic language but *not* without its limitations and frustrations!

Games like Civilization have actually been built using this method though. These provide executables that install all of the necessary modules and libraries as well as the python framework onto a given user's computer. That way, said user is then able to launch the app like any other program without needing any prior knowledge of what Python is. Civ 5 and 6 are pretty successful (you've probably heard of them, at least!) and so this just goes to show us that Python can be used to have a real commercial hit. The sky really is the limit!

More Ways to Distribute Your Apps

Another way you can go about distributing your creations – because of course you are going to want to share them – is to simply release them as .py files. As long as the user has Python installed, they can click on the .py file and it will open a command line and the window to run the app. You can then provide instructions and help on installing Python for those users who don't have it already.

If you want to make an .exe but eventually decide against using PyInstaller, there are many others out there like CXFreeze and like Py2Exe. These all work well depending on how your environment is set up. Unfortunately though, they all do *also* contain a number of stumbling blocks along the way, depending on the versions that you have installed etc.

For these reasons, many people choose to stick with Python 2.7 simply because it has the most support. This will, for the most part, make your life considerably easier and simplify the process of building and exporting games and other apps.

It's really up to you though!

21
Thinking Like a Programmer Part 3

It's time for another of our 'thinking like a programmer' interludes.

At this point, you now know how to make a game, you've built a little animation and you've created a shopping list app. You've even seen how to export these to executables that you can then distribute to other users!

But what if you wanted to make something more practical… like a note-taking tool or a calculator that performs a specific job?

This is where you need to start getting a little more creative and combining the things we've already done in unique ways. You can, for example, combine several of these different things all into one program and that way build yourself a kind of word processor or note taker. This could let you select the file you want from a list and then edit it before saving the changes.

And this is one of the main uses for something like Python. It's time to stop thinking purely in terms of how you can make games in order to sell them and make money, or how to be the next 'Microsoft' with your own massive hit software package. While it's possible, these eventualities are also relatively rare and unlikely!

So instead, think about how you can use Python to build apps and utilities for your *own* benefit. This is what a lot of programmers use coding for – to help themselves get their work done more quickly and to solve unique problems.

We've seen already that a coder will generally *not* write out a piece of code if they can possibly avoid it. Instead, they'll look for an existing module or library that someone else has written and they'll refer to that. This will save them a lot of time and effort, rather than building things from scratch and 'reinventing the wheel'.

This could be seen as 'laziness' on the part of the programmer but rather it is simply efficiency. Why struggle to work out a piece of code when there is a huge, active community out there already helping you?

And that efficiency carries over to *why* many programmers start coding in the first place...

And that is so that they never have to perform a boring, mindless task more than once.

In other words: why input text into a spreadsheet hundreds and hundreds of times over when you could write a simple Python script to do the same thing?

Why have a spreadsheet at all when you can create a program to handle all that data more efficiently?

A smart coder might make an app to help them sort through their email inbox, or they might create an app to help them organize the files more intuitively on their computer.

Often this will involve using more modules or doing other things like that but if it ends up saving you hours and hours in the long run... then isn't it worth it?

One website I highly recommend is called automatetheboringstuff.com/chapter13/. This is a page that will provide you with a bit of detail on two *very* powerful modules that will let you work with PDF files and DocX files. Using both, you can then edit word documents and PDF files and if you are someone who writes for a living in any capacity... well then imagine the amount of time you might potentially be able to save yourself!

In case you haven't quite grasped what I'm saying yet, consider the power of a VAS. A VAS is a 'Virtual Assistant Service' and this is basically an online service that can handle any job you give them. These are companies often based in India and other countries and that can work for a very small amount of money. If you send them a task, whether it is to correct the spelling in a document, or to do some research for you online; they will then handle said job for you for a few dollars.

One high profile news story recently revolved around a man who decided to use one of these services to outsource his entire job! He would receive work from his superiors and then simply get the VAS to do it on his behalf.

Because the VAS company was only charging a dollar or less, he was able to do this work, get paid the normal amount, and then make a big profit! This then mean that he didn't actually do anything all day, he sat at the computer drinking coffee and playing games and got paid a decent salary.

Of course he was eventually caught and got into trouble but technically he was doing nothing wrong! He was being paid to complete certain work and that work was being completed... one way or another.

The point is that you can do this with a piece of software in pretty much any area of your life and end up either earning more, or just saving yourself a ton of time and being able to spend *more* of it doing things that you love.

That is the mindset of a programmer!

22
Building Web Apps

One last final thing you might be interested in is building web-based apps. This is another way to distribute and utilize all your hard work and it will also give you some even more powerful applications, essentially allowing you to build interactive web apps whether they be social sites or powerful utilities. Web apps can be highly profitable as Mark Zuckerberg will attest and they have *countless* uses.

Thankfully, the skills we've learned are relatively easy to take online and we'll look at just enough to get started here.

First, you will be using the Google App Engine framework called Webapp2. To use this, we'll first be downloading the Python SDK (Software Development Kit) from Google here: https://developers.google.com/appengine/downloads#Google_App_Engine _SDK_for_Python.

We're then going to be able to build a 'web server' app right on our own computer, with no need to upload them. This is a good thing, seeing as you may not already have a hosting account etc.

The Basics of Request-Response

Once this is up and running, you'll then be writing a basic program to handle 'requests' to your server. When a visitor types a URL into their browser, the server is going to intercept that request and then use App Engine to look at the configuration file you will have built. It will then use that to know which part of your Python script it needs to deliver. Your app then creates a 'response' page dynamically on the fly and this is delivered to the user and shown in the browser.

First, create a folder on your computer called 'first_app'. Then write a script inside here called 'hello.py' and use the following very basic code:

```
print "Content-Type: text/plain"

print ""

print "Welcome to this webpage"
```

Notice in this instance, we are using Python 2.7 formatting. That is simply for compatibility purpose.

The first statement is the 'header' for the HTTP response and it tells the browser that we're writing in plain text (versus HTML). The second line is simply there to distinguish the header from the body. What follows is what will show in the browser and anything that would normally show in the console will instead show in the browser.

Next you're going to make the configuration file, called 'app.yaml' and this is going to be what tells the browser which pages to display.

Right now, that will be very simple:

```
application: hello

version: 1

runtime: python27

api_version: 1

threadsafe: false

handlers:

- url: /.*

  script: hello.py
```

The line 'runtime:python27' tells the App Engine that it is going to use Python 2.7 to run the app, while the first two lines are just the name and version of the app we've created. Finally, the threadsafe option means that our app can't receive multiple threads at once and the handlers section instructs the engine to display our hello.py when a visitor lands on *any* page of our site. Next, you are going to open this using Google App Engine using a virtual 'local' web server.

Open the program and choose File > Add Existing Application and then choose your first_app folder. You'll add the application using 8080 for the port and choose the application in the main window. And then it should display… you did it!

(Ports basically refer to channels and this allows users to tune in to the right channel on the server. Localhost:8080 means that you're listening to communication from your own computer on port 8080.)

There's a lot more to learn here of course, apart from anything else you need to actually place this on a real server so that it can run as a website! And then you're going to need to know which commands will work in this environment and how to use additional modules.

If you want to work with variables, emails and all kinds of other functionality, then look into the powerful framework called Django. You can learn more at djangoproject.com and the modules can be downloaded through pip using 'pip install django'. A whole world awaits you…

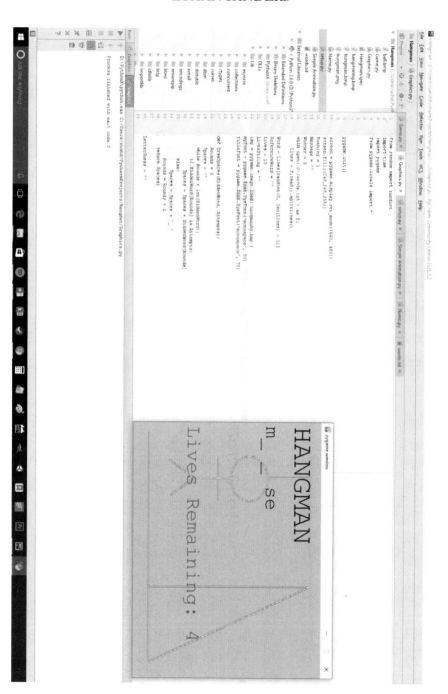

Conclusions

And with that, I must bid you farewell! We've learned a *huge* amount over the course of this book, to the point that you're now able to create entirely functional standalone games with animations, graphics and the ability to read from external files! Why not try building on the Hangman game and then try and make some of your own projects, perhaps something that can help with your daily workflow?

You've learned what it means to think like a programmer more importantly and how to go about expanding your knowledge from these foundations. Maybe that will mean diving into web apps and creating your own 'Software As Service' company.

Whatever the case, just get out there, get experimenting and enjoy the world of programming!

Bonus - Projects for Applying your Python Skills

Below you will find a link to five projects you can get started on today. Applying what you have learnt is the best way to solidify it in your memory.

Try these 5 projects!

http://knightlab.northwestern.edu/2014/06/05/five-mini-programming-projects-for-the-python-beginner/

A YouTube guide to each of these projects is available here too

https://www.youtube.com/playlist?list=PLhP5GzqIk6qsYjU_3tod0nqoWG Xlq9RvF

These projects are just to get you started. There is a wealth of other project ideas and guides available online.

Final Word

Thank you again for downloading this book!

I hope this book was able to help you to start your Python programming journey.

The next step is to apply what you've learnt and stay curious!

Finally, if you enjoyed this book, then I'd like to ask you for a favor, would you be kind enough to leave a review for this book on Amazon? It'd be greatly appreciated! Thank you and good luck

Made in the USA
San Bernardino, CA
23 January 2017